MW00931546

Fire Hydrant Journal

Blank 200 page journal

DiBiasio Publications

Cover design by Brendon DiBiasio

Made in the USA
Las Vegas, NV
18 December 2024

14801937R00115